T0193552

LAVENDER SEEDS

SARAH BAMBA

AuthorHouse™
1663 Liberty Drive
Bloomington, IN 47403
www.authorhouse.com
Phone: 1 (833) 262-8899

*Because of the dynamic nature of the Internet, any web addresses or links contained in this book may have changed
since publication and may no longer be valid. The views expressed in this work are solely those of the author and do not
necessarily reflect the views of the publisher, and the publisher hereby disclaims any responsibility for them.*

*Any people depicted in stock imagery provided by Getty Images are models,
and such images are being used for illustrative purposes only.
Certain stock imagery © Getty Images.*

This book is printed on acid-free paper.

ISBN: 978-1-6655-0011-1 (sc)
ISBN: 978-1-6655-0010-4 (e)

Library of Congress Control Number: 2020918045

Print information available on the last page.

Published by AuthorHouse 09/21/2020

authorHOUSE®

LAVENDER
SEEDS

AN ODE TO THE SPERM DONOR

Oh, sperm donor, you are atrocious
The lack of responsibility inside you
It's intriguing

Oh, sperm donor, you are shadow man
The man with no face
The one who went away

Oh sperm donor as clueless as can be
But not as clueless as me;
The little girl who thought you were coming home

Oh sperm donor how wicked
You horrid disgrace of mankind
Scoundrel in plain site

Oh sperm donor I still need,
Need for you to accept this invite into my life
I'm still waiting on R.S.V.P, d*d

PHOTO CREDIT: SILHOUETTE OF A LONELY MALE, "DESIGNED BY WIRESTOCK / FREEPIK"

SHOE SIZES

How does one leave such big shoes to fill?

How does one who has never been here, to begin with, leave?

Leave me, leave us,?

Now I start to wonder, what would have been different?

Now I start sentences with what if? or how would?

Where would I be, would I be happier. Or am I better off

I don't know; I genuinely don't know.

It hurts not knowing; you begin to find yourself left clueless in a sea of questions.

Now I realize I can't swim, and I start panicking, oh no help!

Now I'm drowning, drowning in a wave that I made for myself.

Drowning inside water, I didn't even know existed.

I can't find the surface; there is no surface to this sea, the sea of the unknown.

You are part of my unknown.

I can sit here for hours, blaming you and call you the underlying cause of all my problems.

All the people I've let go because well, "they all leave anyways."

They all go like him, but he didn't go, he didn't care enough to come, therefore how can he go.

That's right; he can't; he never left here, to begin with.

Remember growing up and still waiting or your arrival, watching at a young age as my little brother got to meet his father.

He spoke to him; he held him.

Now I found myself envying him.

His father leaves, I feel bad. But I still envy, I still crave that lost he got to explore because I've been deprived of that. How sick!

Yeah, trust me, I know!

I now realize there are so many people around me who love me. I can recite it all start the names I lose my breath.

Aunties, Uncles, friends, cousins, brothers, "Totons."

There are much more people

So much who've put me first they are so beautiful, soul-lifting, selfless, a whole community around me filled with beautiful people *sigh*

Breathe in, breathe out

Inhale, exhale

1,2,3,4 count to ten

Slow down you're going to fast

Going at a pace that you can't handle

Remember the most important one the one to remember

My mom, my hero

She has done the impossible, and she stuck with me; she had to become two people. A mother and a father. The man and the woman.

So if I think about no I don't miss him, I don't even know him.

You can't fill the shoe, if you know not the size. So instead of wanting the impossible, I love reality. My reality is what I have at this moment.

The shoe size I know, size eight and half in women's, sometimes and eight depending on the shoe. That size I know that size is my mothers.

AFRICANS HAVE NO WORTH

Africans have no worth
One thing you'll never hear me say is that
I am proud to be African
I hate the way my moms food taste because it's different
One thing I'll never claim is that
I love my deep chocolate melanin toned skin
I can't stand my dark coiled hair
At no time will I proclaim that
I love my African culture
(Now read it backward line by line)

I AM

I am Sarah
I hold the power of my future
I wish I knew which path to head in
I slip up, but so does everyone

I am Matene
I am unique; my culture is like no other
I shine bright in a room with broken lights
I can't be kept hidden or belittled

I am Bamba
I am funny and quirky
I can make even the fiercest lions crack a smile
I laugh to cover up tears and heartbreak

I am Sarah Matene Bamba
I am the only right version of me
I hold myself to a standard set by me
I choose to be the only person who can live my life

LETTER TO THE WORLD

Dear World, I am here
Present
"Smile"
But I'm not always happy
"Don't be that way."
Sorry World
I am not so perfect
What is perfect
Name your definition
Yes World, build your girl
Build your perfect girl
How do you want to start
Which of my unique features do you wish to diminish
Forehead,
Sorry not that, I prefer people to imagine the size of my brain
Yes wonder how smart I am
Body type,
For crying out loud, societies standards are exhausting
World I beg of you
Let young women express themselves
Don't force them to hide due to your standards of "perfect."

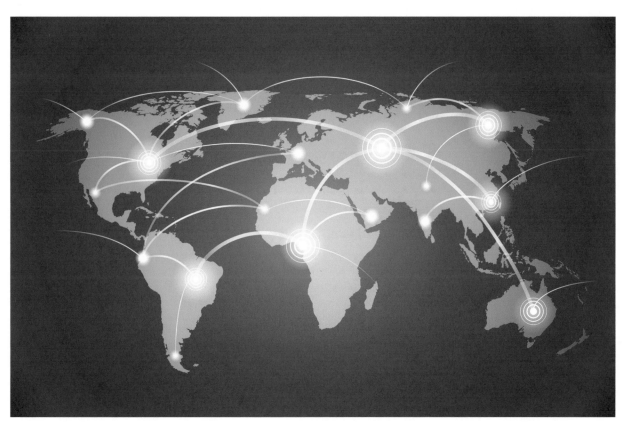

Photo Credit: World map with global technology, "Designed by macrovector / Freepik"

ABC OF ME

Always felt the need to go above expectations.
Believed in not only myself, but those around me
Couldn't fathom why I wasn't the best at everything
Denied myself the right to mess up
Every mistake is documented to prevent repetition.
Failure was simply not an option
Guided to a path of self-doubt and disappointment
Hatred weighed upon me like a boulder
I was honestly at a low point
Justified these actions by my families proudness
Kept every feeling that wasn't joyful bottled up
Life as I knew it was nothing more than just pleasing others
Morning;
Night;
Only served as a reminder that I would repeat this damaging cycle
People around me knew not what was going on
Quilted my life into this bubble I called perfect
Rarely enjoyed anything
Smiled through the hardships
Thought "as long as their proud, that's all that matters."
Under the impression that I was making the best decision
Validation from others was all that kept me going.
Wanting to be the best, craving perfection
Xenial, relationships with others, draining relationship with myself
Yes, it was exhausting, Improvements had to surface
"Zero tolerance for self hate" a new way I choose to live.

PHOTO CREDIT: **TOY BRICKS, DESIGNED BY RACOOL __STUDIO / FREEPIK**

CHOICES

Imagination
Let it run wild and be free
Take the course of your life
Not because I said so;
But cause you are choosing to

DELICACY

Like silence
Like a bubble
A snowflake
An egg yolk
This list
A moment that can be broken by the smallest buzz
A thing that pops more often then it is in its full form
A form of crystalized water which so quickly melts
A membrane which so easily breaks if not handles with care
Fragile
Delicate
A pattern shows in this list
Your life is the silence
It is the bubble
It is the snowflake
It is the yolk
Take care of this life;
For it is the only one you will receive
Do not settle for less than you deserve

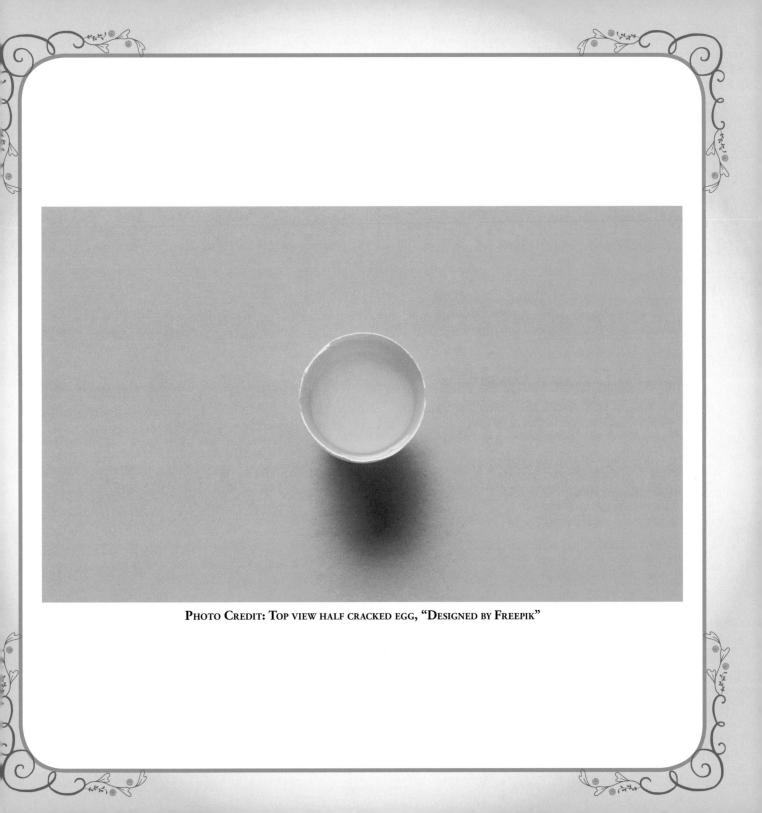

PHOTO CREDIT: TOP VIEW HALF CRACKED EGG, "DESIGNED BY FREEPIK"

ME = HER = SHE

She is unapologetic
Walks on with her head up high
Unbothered
With a growth mindset
She can look in the mirror and just love the view
Loves herself head to toe
She knows there is no such thing as perfect;
But she is her own definition of perfect
Takes all her flaws with an open mind
She is a force to be reckoned with
I aspire to be her
I slowly begin to accept myself
Open up to the idea of being her
I will be referred to as;
She who does not apologize for being herself
She who takes care of feelings;
Doesn't bottle them up
Be her, follow her footsteps
Simply be the best version of me

PHOTO CREDIT: AFRO RETRO GIRL NEON, "DESIGNED BY KATEMANGOSTAR / FREEPIK"

LOVE

Love is something I share with my family
It a feeling, an expression
A way for them to know I care
It's supposed to bring them happiness and joy
I get asked have you loved
Yes I have;
But not in the way you assume
But love is losing its touch
It doesn't give us to same feeling anymore
Love is now a fragile word that causes heartbreak
It's now an illusion put down to trap one in a toxic state of mind
Why has it come down to this
Love used to be beautiful
Now it's stained and feared
Love can you still be the light
Love you are complicated
But I've told once you are discovered Its a miracle.

EFFECT

Bright butterfly
I know you're tired of flapping your wings higher
Poor butterfly the higher you fly
The greater the danger
So you think it's best to clip your wings
Steer clear of the unknown

Small butterfly
You feel too insignificant
Too little to make a difference
Let alone change the world

Butterfly have you heard of your effect
One small butter could cause the end of the world
So one small butterfly could make the world a better place

Colorful butterfly sitting on flower, by erik-karits-2093459, licensed under CC BY 4.0

NEEDS

Have you heard of peace
Desperately needed
Have you heard of hope
Vigorously held on to
Peace and hope can change your world

PHOTO CREDIT: HANDS CONNECTING, "DESIGNED BY FREEPIK"